How 1

Higher

Apprenticeship

by

Joseph Tom Wood

Published by Kevin Wood

ISBN 978-0-9927395-7-7

Introduction

This book contains all the knowledge that I have gained in the process of applying successfully for apprenticeships. It contains the do's and the don'ts of applying, the different stages of the process, and what to expect in interviews and presentations. It also talks about accepting the contract at the end of the process, and what you might expect in the first few weeks of your apprenticeship.

This book is aimed at the people who are applying for higher apprenticeships, that is, level 4 and above. Generally, that's people who are leaving sixth form, but it can also include those who have either taken the first year or two of a degree course - or who've completed a degree in one sector and then decide that they want to move to a different sector.

Apprenticeships are available in a wide range of companies, and cover sectors such as management, accountancy, scientific research, agriculture, engineering... In fact, there isn't a single area where apprenticeships are not available.

You have to know how to find apprenticeships, and apply for them. You need to know how to get through the elimination process and attend interviews. You need to know how to do a presentation and shine in team work exercises.

If you're thinking, "I don't even know where to start or where to begin at getting an apprenticeship", this book will give you helpful pointers in the right direction.

Read through this book and take notes on all the information - there is a lot to cover.

I wish you the best on the start of your journey.

Why do an apprenticeship?

Two reasons: Industry experience and money.

Industry experience is probably self-explanatory. All apprenticeships include a large portion of actually "doing the job". Once you have completed your apprenticeship, you will hit the ground running, and be producing useful work from day one. At the end of an apprenticeship, you're practically guaranteed a job. On the other hand, it is often reckoned that it's six months before you get useful work out of a fresh graduate, regardless of how smart they are. This isn't because of the quality of the teaching at university, it's because of the lack of industry experience, and how learning is applied in the real world. Apprentices are in the real world from the beginning.

As for the money, well, consider the cost of being a student.

At 2022 prices, tuition on a degree course is £9250 per year. Accommodation costs vary, but for a basic room with en-suite bathroom and shared kitchen, you're probably looking at £7100 per year (it doesn't get much better when you move out of halls). Then you have to eat, wash, do your laundry – and that's at least £60 a week. Add in the cost of paper, printer ink, travel, clothing… your weekly costs are now edging up to £100 a week, so let's hope your parents are prepared to pay your mobile phone bill. And don't forget you'll probably need a TV license.

Assuming that you never go out for a drink, or get takeaways, make all your own food and live like a hermit, you can probably get by on £20,000 per year.

This means that by the end of a three year degree course unless you have a rich uncle somewhere, you will be at least £60,000 in debt.

Contrast this with an apprenticeship, where it is not unusual for a company to <u>pay you</u> that amount to do a degree.

It also has to be mentioned that if you have taken the BTEC rather than the A-level route, apprenticeships can sometimes be more accessible than university. Suppose you had a BTEC Level 3 Extended Diploma with D*D*D* - that gives you the same number of UCAS points as someone with three A-levels at A*A*A*, right? Yes, but… Universities will tend to prefer the A-level candidate, because they know exactly what they're getting, whereas they have to unpack each BTEC course to see what modules the student has been taught. Companies taking on apprentices are only interested in whether or not you're the best candidate for the job, so have to take a more individual approach. A-level or BTEC doesn't matter to them.

Does all this make it a no-brainer? Not quite.

Bear in mind that as an apprentice you will be working eight hour days, then going home and studying. Weekends? What are they?

Meanwhile, your student friends will be quaffing ale at the Student Union bar.

Yes, you get paid. Yes, you get industry experience. But you also have to be prepared to work hard – very hard – and be good at organising your life.

If you can accept that, then an apprenticeship is an excellent choice.

Finding an apprenticeship

Before you start looking at apprenticeship adverts, a quick explanation of what "Levels" are. You will see that an apprenticeship will be described as a "Level 5 apprenticeship", or a "Level 6". What this tells you is the kind of qualification you will have at the end of the course. Level 4 is the level above A-levels (for example, Higher National Certificate or HNC), level 5 is the next level up (Higher National Diploma – HND), level 6 is degree with honours (say, BSc (hons)), and level 7 is a Masters degree. Naturally, the higher the level, the more difficult it is to get onto the course. Also, if you've just taken A-levels (which are level 3) you don't want to be looking at a level 2 (GCSE equivalent) apprenticeship.

There are a number of ways you can look for an apprenticeship. Generally you need to start looking from September onwards the year before you want to start an apprenticeship. They are advertised throughout the year but a lot are advertised between October and January. So be ready.

The most obvious one is through school or college career events and careers advisors. Some schools give out The Times Top 100 Graduate Employers guide. This lists many employers and how they employ people and their preferred route. It also gives an estimated starting salary. This book is republished every year (so the ISBN number will change) so you know it will have current information.

Careers fairs are a good way of meeting potential employers and finding apprenticeship schemes. Networking like this may not lead to an immediate choice but could potentially be a stepping stone. For example, you could meet an employer that may not be quite up your street but who knows of a better fit you could try. It gives you a chance to ask questions and take leaflets to research on the internet later. The more you know about a company the more the informed your choice.

Another method of finding an apprenticeship is through an online job website such as Indeed. There are quite a few different websites like this you could register with. You can also create an 'alert', which means you could put your level of apprenticeship down (such as level 4 or degree), subject (such as biochemistry or engineering) and location. That way, you will automatically get an email with the job match. The wider the choice location the better but bear in mind it's always a balancing act. If the job is at the other end of the country, you won't be able to live with family, so you will need to be sure that you can afford to live on the salary in that location. Similarly, if you have family commitments, such as being a carer, you will need something closer to home. Be realistic - however don't set your sights too low or narrow your scope too much, as you can always turn something down later if you change your mind.

There is also UK Government Career Finder website:

https://nationalcareers.service.gov.uk

Here you can get information and chat on line to an adviser.

There is also the UK Government Apprenticeship website

https://www.gov.uk/apply-apprenticeship

Again this allows you to add filters and create a list that suits you better.

One drawback to using online job websites is that not all companies use these websites to advertise their apprenticeships. However by following what comes into your 'inbox' you will start to get a feel for what is out there and the range of salaries and locations they are in.

You can also find apprenticeships by quite simply researching a company directly using a search engine. If you are interested in being an electrician or scientist you could look at what companies are out there. Follow the links to their websites and then to the jobs and see if there are any apprenticeship routes. This method had the best results for me personally. Doing this often gives you an insight into the company, when they are likely to 'open their applications' and the process they follow. Many of these large companies have a specific time they open up their applications and are often on a "first come first served" basis if they are inundated with applicants. Some will say, "Apprenticeship applications open at the beginning of October". This means you can set up a reminder on your phone or calendar to recheck the site at that time and start the application straight away. That way you don't miss your chance.

Finally, family and friends and general networking also gives you an insight into what companies are out there. What do your friends' parents' do for a job? Is it in a similar field to where you want to go? What were their experiences of how they got into their positions etc.? Depending on your social circle, this may be limiting yourself or may give you food for thought.

Here's a couple of websites where you will find apprenticeships discussed:

The Student Room has a lot of general discussion (and some noise) about most educational topics, including apprenticeships.

https://www.thestudentroom.co.uk

Rate My Apprenticeship has discussion from people who have been, or who are apprentices, and can give you a particular insight into companies you might apply for. They also advertise apprenticeships, so it's a valuable resource in more ways than one:

https://www.ratemyapprenticeship.co.uk

However a word of warning: Don't be influenced too much by other people. This is YOUR choice and your career.

You should also look at the final destination of the apprenticeship. Once qualified, is it what you want to do? Does it pay OK? Would you have to move?

Glass Door can help you answer these questions:

https://www.glassdoor.co.uk/index.htm

As with all the suggestions of websites above, Glass Door isn't the only website that provides information like this – it's just a starting point.

As an observation, it seems that the greater the perceived prestige of the apprenticeship, the lower the wage. Perhaps this is because they tend to have a high level of skill and interest. This is just an observation from past experience in the field I went for so take at face value.

A last point: if an aerospace company is asking for manufacturing engineers, do not think that it might provide a way into becoming a test pilot. They advertise for apprentice manufacturing engineers because they want manufacturing engineers. If they wanted test pilots, they'd ask for test pilots. Similarly with car manufacturers and racing car drivers. It might sound silly, but people do ask these questions in group sessions.

Here's a basic check list to go through when you are looking at these adverts for the apprenticeships:

- Does the job description match what you want to do?

- Have you got the right qualifications with the right grades?

- Is it the level of apprenticeship you wanted?

- Where are you studying? What University or college?

- What experience are they looking for?

- What is their salary?

- Where will you end up once qualified? What might your progression be? Will you be offered a job for example?

Disability Confident Employers

A Disability Confident Employer is useful if you have a disability, as the people in the decision making process will have had additional training to ensure that the recruitment process is fair. In some cases, this may mean that you get an automatic interview. This does not mean that they will positively discriminate in favour of disabled people. It means that everyone will get the same chance. If you are not disabled, do not think you can get a better shot by saying that you are – it will be spotted, and will guarantee you don't get the position. But if you do have a disability, then say so. The adjustments are there for a reason.

The Government website is especially helpful for identifying Disability Confident Employers. It also allows you to set this as a filter in your search criteria.

If you do have a disability, it is not necessary to restrict yourself to Disability Confident Employers, but at least you know that they will give you a level playing field.

Applying

Basics

Keep a record of what you are applying for. Print or save their job description as it often disappears from the website after the application deadline has passed. You may need to refer back to it for an assessment later and it's a bit embarrassing if you have forgotten the job description of the job you are applying for. Keep all the job descriptions in one place, whether it's on a computer, or printed out. Discard any job descriptions where you get rejected so you can see where you are.

Expect to apply for 20+ apprenticeships.

I will repeat that, because this isn't like applying for a university place, where you list five universities, and then shortlist two – apprenticeships require a different mind-set.

Expect to apply for 20+ apprenticeships.

That sounds like an eye-watering number of applications, but with the right approach you can reduce the workload considerably.

Why do you need to do so many applications?

A university course that has 14 applicants for each place is considered a tough one to get into.

An apprenticeship scheme that has 140 applicants for each place is considered easy. For a top-flight degree level apprenticeship, you can expect to be competing with 50,000 applicants or more. This is not exaggeration for effect – it is the simple truth. Competition for apprenticeship places at all levels is much fiercer than for the equivalent academic routes.

Do not think for one moment that this means an apprenticeship is unobtainable – far from it. But don't expect to only have to apply for one or two, and make sure that you meet all the criteria the employer asks for (qualifications, etc.) before applying. If you check you meet all the criteria before applying, you've probably already put yourself in the top 25% of candidates.

When applying for that many positions, it is clear you need to have a record of what you've applied for, and what stage you've got to with each application. A spread sheet like the one on the next page might be a good option here, or even just a hand-written list. Make sure that you keep it up to date, though, otherwise it will be useless. Properly maintained, it will give you an over view of what you have applied for.

Apprenticeship	Date	Applied	1st stage	2nd stage	Interview	Outcome	Notes
1.The Good Company plc Degree apprenticeship	10/10/22	✓	✓	-	Awaiting interview in March		£18500 4 years Stevenage
2.Another Good Company plc Degree apprenticeship	11/10/22	✓	✓			✖	£19000 4 years Bristol

A sample spreadsheet for recording apprenticeship applications

Curriculum Vitae (CV)

Your Curriculum Vitae (CV) - which you will hear referred to on American shows as a Resume - is vitally important. "Curriculum Vitae" translates from Latin to "The Course of Life", and quite simply, it lists everything that you have done. This means what schools you've been to, what qualifications you have (or are studying for), work experience that you've gained, hobbies and any awards you may have received.

CVs need time to get right and they really need to be tailored to the job you are going for. Have a number of them ready but be carefully how you name them in your folders on the computer. For example CV 1, CV 2 is fine for the succession of CV's you write but you don't want to call it that on application form. Rename it to your name (for example, "Joe_Bloggs_CV.docx") is probably the best thing to do. Then when you up load it, it will say your name clearly on the box.

Application forms

Sometimes application forms have an auto fill, which takes information from your CV and uses it to fill in details on the form. This can save time but be careful as you still have to check everything. Sometimes they can take odd bits of information from your CV and put them into strange places. Make sure it makes sense, and especially ensure your address is correct. Often you will find that it auto fill has put the house name instead of the area or county instead of the village and odd details like that.

Another important thing to look out for early on is whether the application form can save as you go or whether you have to finish it in one sitting. If you do have to finish it in one sitting, choose your time carefully as they can take an hour or more to do right. Some are timed and you have to log back in, again check this before you start if you can. The problem is that you don't find out if the form can be saved until after you have started.

The majority now have a save button after each page or section. This means you can really think about how you fill it in. Either way have a word document open so you can type in your blurb for the boxes and count the characters for the character limit if it has one. It gives you a chance to check spelling and also reflect on what you are trying to say. Once happy, cut and paste into the appropriate box on the form. When you do it this way, I would spend an extra minute typing or cutting and pasting the actual question on the word document too and then you can save this for later knowing the question and answer you put down. This is also useful when applying for more multiple apprenticeships. Why re-invent the wheel?

However, a word of caution: if you do that you still have to re read and tailor it to the next application form. For example – "I always wanted to work for The Really Good Company plc because it's dynamic and at the forefront of innovation". If you copy and paste this into your application for Another Good Company plc, then do not expect a positive response. Even without mistakes as obvious as this, the chances are that you will still want to tweak your answers to be as specific to the company as possible. That said, it does still save time and is good for those more generic applications. It also allows you to see what has worked and what has not. You can check your hit rate for getting through to the next round in the selection process.

Here are some examples of typical questions that you might encounter on an application form:

- Please tell us about any work experience you have undertaken and/or any hobbies and interests that relate to the scheme you are applying to.

- Please can you explain why you're interested in the position you're applying for and why you think you would be great candidate for the role?

- What are your main strengths? Please provide examples of when you've demonstrated your strengths.

- What skills would you like to improve during this apprenticeship?

And then there is this old favourite:

- Why you? Why would we choose you?

Generally speaking, you should try to sound dynamic and enthusiastic in answering the questions. Mention outside interests and volunteering if it seems appropriate. Don't go overboard and gush – but equally, make sure you sell yourself as best you can.

These questions often have a word limit (say, 250 or 500 words), or sometimes a character limit (say, 1000 characters). If there is a character limit, then be aware that word processors such as Microsoft Word often don't count spaces when they give you a character count, so double check this. If there is a limit on the length of your answer, don't exceed it. I know it might be tempting to try and squeeze in that little bit extra information about some brilliant project you did – but would you give an apprenticeship to someone who can't follow basic instructions?

Many application forms will want evidence of qualifications uploaded too. Make sure all your certificates (GCSE, A- level, BTEC, etc.) have been scanned in and saved on a computer and you have access to them. The most important ones appear to be Maths and English GCSE. If you do not have a copy of your certificate, then you can request a "Certified Statement of Results" from your exam board. If you took the exam a few years ago, it is possible that the exam board may no longer exist. In this case, you can still get the information you need. Check this Government website for details:

https://www.gov.uk/replacement-exam-certificate/if-your-old-exam-board-no-longer-exists

It's likely that you won't have taken all your exams when you fill in your application form (for example, if you're taking A-levels), or completed all your course work (for example, on a BTEC course). That's not a problem – put down your predicted grades. Your teacher will be able to help you with this. To state the obvious, don't be tempted to inflate the grades you're likely to get. It will only bring your grief, especially if then you don't get the grades.

Once the application is done, many give you an opportunity to review it before hitting the big send button. This is worth going over even though you might have had enough at that stage. Many a mistake can be picked up here and corrected.

What Happens After You Submit Your Application

Very often, your application will be rejected at the first stage.

Don't worry about it.

That first rejection can feel like a disaster, especially if it's an apprenticeship that you really had set your heart on. It is important to realise that it doesn't mean that you did anything wrong, or that you're not smart enough, or that you haven't got the "right stuff". It's just the way apprenticeships work, which is why I said that you had to expect to apply for 40+ apprenticeships.

The problem is that it's never possible to know exactly what a company is looking for. In fact, even if you manage to get talking to some of the people involved in the decision making, the answer often comes down to, "I know the right candidate when I see them". It's not a tick-box list of criteria.

So even when the rejections start piling up, keep ploughing on, because one day you will get an e-mail asking you to move on to the next stage.

The Next Stage

Every company works a little differently, and some selection processes have more stages than others. Don't be surprised if a company misses out one of the stages here, or does things in a strange order. It is possible that they might include a stage that I haven't covered, although what you see here should give you a good idea what to expect. Whoever you're applying to will be doing things a certain way for a reason. Perhaps it's because past experience has shown them that a particular test adds value to their recruitment process, or perhaps there are other factors in play. For example, many changed their selection process during the Pandemic and the restrictions Lockdown imposed.

If something is not listed here, or in a strange order, then that's fine. Be adaptable – after all, that's a commonly prized attribute in a would-be apprentice.

Tests

The tests are usually Maths, English and Non-Verbal Reasoning (NVR). Sometimes there is also a Data test or an Ethics test. The level of the test will depend on the type of apprenticeship you're applying for, and the level of the apprenticeship. It should go without saying, but a bit of revision is always helpful. If you've spent the last couple of years doing science-based A-levels, it's likely that your English Language skills are a little rusty. Similarly, if you've gone down a Humanities route, you may need to brush up on your Maths. NVR is not taught as standard in school, but (because NVR often forms part of the selection process for the 11+ test) you can get practice books in outlets such as WH Smiths. They are also available online. I am unaware of any suitable means of revising for a Data test, but it is always worth searching online for more information.

Perhaps it is worth noting that they will only expect you to obtain a suitable score in the tests for the role that you are applying for. If you are applying for a Human Resource position, for example, it probably isn't necessary to be able to solve complex mathematical problems in your head. The testing will be appropriate for the position you are applying for.

Many of these tests are performed online, and they

can take anywhere from ten minutes to an hour or more for each test. Sometimes you will be told in advance how long a test will take, but just as often you don't find out until you've started the test. Therefore, do the obvious things to give yourself the best chance. Choose a time to do the test when you know you've got an hour or more free, and will get some peace and quiet. Ensure your internet connection is good, and you're not going to be caught out by flaky WiFi. Never try to do these tests using a phone – the test just aren't designed to be used on a phone (and tablets aren't much better for this), and you'll be putting yourself at a disadvantage. If you don't have access to a PC or laptop, then ask for help at school, or go to a public library.

Maths

The maths test could be GCSE or A-level standard, it could be pure or applied or further maths. With all these tests you really don't know what you will get until you start the test. Read up to the highest level you know, but don't forget to remind yourself of the basics. When was the last time you multiplied two fractions together? Or worried about how high a tree was when you were standing 10 metres away? It might be years since you last answered questions like these.

Generally, the tests won't exactly fit into the

syllabus of any one exam. This is a deliberate choice, as it tests how good you are at mathematics, rather than how good you are at maths exams – a subtly different point.

English

The English test typically covers basic skills such as spelling, punctuation and grammar. In these tests you will want to be careful of spoken English and written English, as these tests are all based around written English as you would say it out loud. It could be something you aren't used to saying or might say in a different way. Typical tests might be to add punctuation to a passage of text, or to correct spelling mistakes. You might also be asked to check and correct tenses (past, present, future), or look for appropriate word use (to, too and two – or if you're unlucky, ensure, insure and assure).

Non-verbal reasoning

Whereas with Maths, you can either add numbers together or not, and in English, a comma is always a comma, NVR is more about identifying patterns and solving problems with logic. Typically, this is done with visual problems, but (especially in the age of online tests) it can include (for example) sound and other methods.

You may get these as the classic multiple choice question, or (and this is something of a growth industry) the company you've applied to may have contracted this out to another company specialising in this kind of test.

If it has been contracted out, then rather than a multiple choice test it might take the form of a game, or puzzle solving. The company doing the testing (there are several) will explain beforehand how by playing a game, it will enable them to test over 7000 data points, thus providing a complete and consistent analysis of your personality.

Often, they will give you a feedback form, detailing your results from the test, which is nice. The kind of thing that they look at is whether you are a leader or a follower, whether you are an innovator or prefer following an established path.

In practice, the same test from the same company can give different results every time. I have had four quite different results for the same test.

If you do get the computerised interactive type of test, then don't try and guess what they want from you. Each company will have a different profile that they believe will be the best fit for their company. You can look at the feedback and drive yourself nuts thinking, "Well, perhaps if I had done this instead of that…" – it doesn't work like that. This kind of test is something that you just have to accept for what it is.

The multiple choice type of test, however, is one where there is a direct score, and it is something that you can practice for. Obviously, if you can practice for it, then you should.

Data tests

A Data test is another kind of test that you might be presented with, especially for high-end apprenticeships or large companies. They might be called another name by a particular company, but the format is the same.

You are presented a screen with some information on it. This might be a table giving figures like turnover, profit, sales and similar data for several companies. It might be a series of graphs. It might be a page of text describing some aspect of several companies. You will then be asked a series of questions about the data – for example, "Was the gross profit of Company A in year 3 more or less than the combined gross profit of Company B and Company C in year 4?"

The object of these tests is to see how good you are at extracting complex data from limited information, and often, also to see how good you are at interpolating data (for example, "Does the data suggest that Company A has improved its market position?"

Unfortunately, there seems to be limited resources for practicing this kind of test. The best advice I can give here is to make sure that you can read tables and graphs, and familiarise yourself with basic business terms such as Turnover, Gross Profit, Net Profit etc. (that is not an exhaustive list of terms, just an indication).

Ethics

This seems to be becoming more popular. Essentially, companies with a good ethical standard do better in the long term. They are ultimately more stable and make more money. Companies with poor ethical standards may make a quick buck, but not consistently, and generally aren't around for that long. It doesn't take much to work out that a company's best strategy is to maintain a high ethical standard. If you want to learn more on why this is, then I suggest you research it. It is too large a subject to explore here, but there is a vast amount of literature available and the results are conclusive.

The ethics tests typically give you a scenario, such as "Ted works for a construction company, and has responsibility for assigning contracts. One of his contractors offers him tickets to a football match when a contract is due for renewal. Should he accept the tickets?"

With these tests, the thing is to not only look at whether or not a situation is right or wrong, but also whether it might have the <u>appearance</u> of looking wrong. Often the appearance to outside spectators can be just as important as the reality. In the example above, the answer would be that Ted should not accept the tickets, because it could give the <u>appearance</u> of bribery to get a new contract, even if it was quite innocent.

The essential with ethics tests is to stick to the rules, and not take short cuts – which is a good principle in any case.

Video Interviews

Since the Pandemic and Lockdowns, video interviews have become more common. At the time of Lockdown face-to-face interviews were obviously not possible, and afterwards, people realised that there were many benefits to video interviews. Specifically, candidates did not need to travel, which saved money and reduced CO_2 emissions.

There are two forms of video interviews – pre-recorded, and live – but some aspects are common to both.

The Basics

If you have the option of choosing a time for the interview (typically this only applies to pre-recorded interviews), then make sure it is a time where you can be sure that you won't be disturbed.

Dress right for the interview – formal professional is the key here. Make sure that you are wearing professional looking clothes, pay attention to your personal grooming (hair brushed, shave if appropriate). It doesn't matter if the person interviewing you is dressed in a dirty T-shirt – that's their prerogative. You make sure that you are dressed right.

Ensure that you have a neutral background. I used to shift half the furniture in the room so that I could have a blank wall behind me. What you don't want is anything that might be disturbing to the interviewers. Don't use the background function available in Teams or Zoom to replace whatever is behind you – that can cause strange artefacts which can be disconcerting. Anything that might distract from you and what you're saying is a bad thing, and must be eliminated.

Make sure your sound and video work correctly beforehand. It might seem obvious, but it's surprising how often something that worked the night before fails on the day.

A headset with built-in microphone always seems acceptable.

Using a laptop's built-in speakers and microphone is not so good, but also seems acceptable.

If you have some complex boom-microphone gaming-style arrangement, ensure that it is not visible in the video. It doesn't matter how much it costs, or how good it is, it can be a distraction to the interviewers.

The best seat to sit on is one that won't be visible in the video. You might have a really comfortable high-backed racing style seat – but again, it can be a distraction. I used a dining chair.

Always research the company before any kind of interview. It is standard practice to ask a candidate what they know about a company. They might also ask you about issues specific to their industry. For example, a pharmaceutical company might ask how you feel about vivisection. Be ready for those kind of questions. "Er, um, I don't really know," is probably not the best answer.

If you have said that you are disabled on your application, then you will be asked if any adjustments are necessary. Be honest. If you need something, then ask, but equally, don't try and play the sympathy card, because people will spot that. You know what you need, make sure that others are also aware. Remember, this is about ensuring there is a level playing field.

Remember – whatever you do, interviews are all about you, and presenting yourself in the best possible light. You must ensure that nothing will distract the interviewers from this.

Pre-recorded Video Interviews

These give you the chance to record a series of short videos in response to questions. There are some variations, such as the amount of time allowed between the questions being asked, and having to record the answer, or whether or not you get the chance to re-record your answer, but the fundamentals are the same.

You are asked a question, and then, after a short pause (anything from a few seconds to a minute) you have to record your answer. Be aware that recording typically starts automatically.

The key to this is to print off <u>all</u> the blurbs that you've done for the applications that you've submitted. Have them readily accessible, but out of sight of your camera. Once the question has been asked, nine times out of ten you will have the answer in the blurb you've done for an application. Maybe it's a question you didn't have to answer for <u>this</u> company (why would they ask you the same thing twice?) but there's an good chance you will have the answer already written out from something you've done for <u>another</u> company.

The tenth time, you just have to come up with the answer on the spot.

Live Video Interviews

These are exactly the same as a face-to-face interview, except it's over video link. Look over the basics for video interviews, make sure that you are ready.

Always, always before a live video interview, read over what you said in your application form. You will be asked questions about it. Other than that, there's not much can be said – or rather, it's the same as any other interview, of which there is a vast quantity of information available.

If you can get interview practice at college or school, then always take that opportunity. It can really help.

Presentations

If you are asked to do a presentation, then it is a big deal. A good presentation may not guarantee you'll get the apprenticeship (although it's a big help), but you can be sure that a bad one will lose it.

Not all companies ask for a presentation, but most do.

The presentation is typically required to be about the business, or a subject related to the business. Sometimes they might ask you to do a presentation about something that you are interested in.

After you have given your presentation, you will be asked questions about it,

Generally, you are given between one and two weeks to prepare the presentation. In this time, you will have to come up with a presentation and practice it until you know it by heart, and then some more until you are sick of it. You will also practice it in front of friends and family, and get their feedback on it. After each practice, you will tweak it until it is perfect. Don't forget to get anyone sitting through your presentation to ask you questions about it.

Presentations are timed, so you will be told to do a five minute presentation, or a ten minute presentation – do not go over the limit, because they might cut you short. Checking that you can keep the presentation within the required time is part of practicing.

The presentation may be done via video-link (Teams, Zoom, etc.) or it may be done face-to-face. If it is done via video-link, then it will almost always be done using PowerPoint.

Be aware that it is common practice for companies to request PowerPoint presentations a day or so before the presentation is due. This may affect your preparation timing. There are two reasons for requesting the presentation in advance. The first is so the interviewers can familiarise themselves with the material, and form relevant questions. The second is so that they can run it through an anti-plagiarism program, to make sure you didn't just copy stuff of the internet. Needless to say, copy/paste from Wikipedia is an auto-fail. Yes, look stuff up, but always draw things out of the material you research, and put it in your own words.

If you are doing the presentation face-to-face, then you're not limited to a PowerPoint (unless they specify PowerPoint, of course). There are many options in this regard, but people tend to forget them, as it is easy to just think "Presentation = PowerPoint".

For example, you could get a series of A3 boards, and put things on them. One of the advantages of this is that you can stick extra little diagrams onto the boards with Velcro as you're talking. This makes it more interactive, If you're good at drawing, then perhaps this might help (although be aware that the timescales are tight – you can't spend two weeks on one drawing).

If you have a model that you have made, or some physical object that is appropriate to the presentation, make sure they see it. If it's a face-to-face presentation, it can then be passed amongst the presentation panel, and can be useful for stimulating questions. This only applies for certain kinds of jobs. It might be appropriate for an engineering apprenticeship, but coming up with something like this for an accountancy apprenticeship would be a bit of a head-scratcher. The key point here is that things should be appropriate to the apprenticeship you're apply for.

What won't work is to think that you can just stand in front in panel and talk to them. This makes it look like you haven't tried. And the truth is, if you haven't prepared any material for the presentation, then you really haven't tried.

Although methods other than PowerPoint can come across really well, very often you will still have to use it. It might be because that's what is specified, or perhaps because it's a video presentation. I'm not going to give a detailed style guide on how to produce a good PowerPoint presentation here – there are many such style guides available, written by people with far more expertise in this area than me.

Instead, I'll just cover a few basics, to help you avoid some of the more common mistakes.

Title Slide

The title slide is just meant to announce whatever you are presenting. It should have the topic that you are presenting, and your name. It doesn't need to be clever, in fact, basic is better.

Background

Every slide should have a background, and the background should be the same for every slide. The background has to be something that relates to the topic throughout. It should be something that isn't too bold because otherwise it might obscure the text. You can do this by turning up the opacity of the image up and down until it looks right.

References

It is fine to quote small bits of information, or use diagrams and pictures that someone else has produced, as long as – and this is really important – you credit the source. This is called referencing. Any material that you use from elsewhere, you should reference. The very last slide should have a list of references. There are various ways of referencing, but the most common one is called Harvard Referencing. Harvard Referencing is very easy to look up on the internet, and covers all kinds of things from books and journals to web pages. The most common thing you're likely to want to reference is a web page, so I'll give you the format for that:

Author (date). Available at: web page URL (Accessed date)

For example:

J. Wood (2022). Available at: **https://jwood.com/samplereference.html** (Accessed 01 September 2022)

If you really don't need to use references (perhaps it's a topic that you're an expert on, and the background picture is one that you took yourself), then don't put them in.

Talking Points

Do not just read the slide. The panel of people you are talking to can do that for themselves. You need to flesh out the contents of the slide.

And always make sure you stay on topic.

Presentation Time

You can't go over the time that has been specified, so don't put too many slides in. As a rule of thumb, reckon that five minutes is at most eight slides. This means forty seconds (roughly) per slide. Add in a title page, and a final page with references (you don't need to read out the references, just leave them on screen to show that you've done it), and that's a total of ten pages for a five minutes presentation.

Don't forget – when you're practising, time yourself with a stopwatch.

Flashy Effects

In some schools, they get you to use lots and lots of flashy effect, like animations, slide in, slide out, and stuff like that. Don't use them. This is not school, and there is always a suspicion that the effects are being used to distract from lack of content.

Sample Good slide

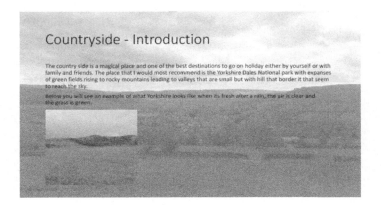

- Not clustered - easy to read
- Image with title
- Font is easy to read in a standard type face
- Good flow to read and explain to the interviewers

Sample Bad Slide

- Cluttered, with too much text
- Pictures dumped in at random, overlapping text
- Cannot be assimilated easily
- Uses the singular of "Thing" in the title instead of the plural

Face-To-Face

Now that we're past the Pandemic and Lockdowns, companies are moving back to having at least some time face-to-face with candidates. Video is great, and it enabled people to carry on doing at least some things during Lockdown, but it has its limits. There are all kinds of non-verbal clues in a person's body language that just don't carry over as well on video. The bottom line is that we have millions of years of evolution that has taught us how to interpret these signs, but we've only had video conferencing for a few years. We are better at judging people face-to-face.

However, it is more expensive for a company to do the face-to-face thing, so if you get the invite, it is a big deal. It's not a guarantee of an apprenticeship, but you're onto the last stage. Companies vary a lot, of course, but it's not uncommon for them to take between a third and a half of candidates following face-to-face sessions.

The event might not take place on a company site – for example, there might be security restrictions, or the site might not have the facilities necessary. In this case they will probably hire a hotel or conference centre for the day. However, if it is possible, then it will be held onsite. At this stage, the nature of the recruitment process changes. It is no longer only a process of "Are you good enough?", although there is still an element of that. It's about whether you'll fit in with the company. That means them showing you what they're really like to work for. Hence, if possible, they'll get you onsite.

As always, every company does things their own way, but face-to-face is generally either a half-day or full-day session. It will include obvious evaluation points, such as interviews, but it will likely also include the opportunity to chat to people who are currently on the apprenticeship scheme. If the face-to-face takes place at one of the company's sites, then you will probably get a tour.

If you have told the company that you are disabled, then the comments I made in the section on video interviews apply, but more so. You will be asked about any adjustments that you may require. Be honest. Especially be honest if you are likely to have difficulties such as becoming excessively tired due to the nature of the day. You might want to cover this up, thinking that a show of weakness will prejudice the company against you. Quite the opposite. If you're honest about your problems, then they will be able to work with you. If you try and hide things, then you could potentially put people at risk, and certainly you will place the company in an awkward position. Always be honest.

At these sessions, you will meet other candidates. Group sizes vary, but it seems that most companies will take candidates in groups of eight to twelve at a time for these events. Of course, you will be very concerned about your own performance and how you present yourself, but it is important not to hard shoulder the other candidates. If you're successful, then these guys will be your colleagues for the next few years, and possibly beyond. If you're not seen to be getting on with them, then it won't look great. For that matter, if one of them starts to give you the treatment, then just smile politely, and move on. Be open and friendly at all times. By the end of the day, you should feel the corners of your mouth aching from all the constant smiling.

If, by nature, you're the introverted, "quiet one at the back" kind of person, this process can be very intimidating. Don't worry. The interviewers will be experienced people who know that the person with the biggest mouth is not always the best employee. Make sure you shine with things like your presentation and interview, and you will do fine.

Sometimes, the company will give you a dress-code for the session, for example, "casual business", or "smart business". Do what they say – and dress up from what they say rather than down. If you're wearing a shirt and tie, you can always remove your tie. If you're in jeans and a T-shirt while everyone else is wearing smart business suits, then you're stuck. Bear in mind that smartly dressed or not, you need to be comfortable if you're to give your best performance. Also it is possible that a team building exercise may require you to get down on your hands and knees. If this is the case, then normally they will offer you overalls. If not, then don't worry about it – you can always take your suit to the dry cleaners afterwards.

Two practicalities:

First, if the event takes place over lunch time, then check if you need to bring a packed lunch. Some places provide lunch, and some don't, and it's not always down to the size of the company. Some quite major players expect you to provide your own. If they don't tell you, then it's worth asking. If lunch is provided and you have an allergy, then tell them. You don't want to finish the day with an anaphylactic episode.

Second, if the face-to-face session is a long way away, then it is worth considering staying overnight the night before. I have got up at three in the morning to travel 200 miles for an eight o'clock start, and it isn't much fun. Naturally, even a cheap hotel can be a significant cost, but if the option is available to you then give it some thought.

Remember – they will watch everything you do from when you set foot on their premises until you leave.

Here's some of the things that might happen:

Interview

Most of this has been covered in the section on video interviews. It's a little different face-to-face. In a video interview, they can't see if you're mauling a stress ball off-camera. You have to be aware of yourself a little more. Still, this is something that can be practiced beforehand, with friends and families, or with teachers and lecturers.

Presentation

As discussed before, it is probable that if you are doing a PowerPoint presentation, they will already have requested the file from you. If not, then you will have to take a copy of the file with you on a USB memory stick. If the instructions you are given don't make this clear, then ask. Even if they have asked you to email the file across, take a copy on a USB memory stick anyway, because stuff happens. In fact, take two memory sticks, in case you lose one or it breaks or something. And put the second memory stick in a different pocket. Don't forget to check that the file works after you've put it on the memory stick. This is absolutely serious. Can you imagine having put all the work into getting this far, and then losing it because you didn't bother giving the memory stick one last check?

If you're doing a presentation with, for example, a flip-chart, then it is reasonable to expect them to provide the facilities for you to do the presentation. If the worst comes to the worst, then one of the panel can always hold up your display while you talk. If you have taken a physical object with you, such as a model, then give the panel members the opportunity to handle it (unless it is especially fragile, but you get the idea).

Don't be daunted if you see that someone else has got what looks like a really great presentation – focus on doing your presentation as well as possible. Besides, someone else's presentation may look slick, but if it doesn't have the content, then it's worthless.

Team Test

Some form of teamwork test is a standard feature of face-to-face sessions. By the time you do the team test, you may have known your team five minutes or five hours.

The basics still apply. Don't cold-shoulder anyone. Treat other people how you would want to be treated.

When you arrive in the room and are given the parameters of the test, remember this isn't a test of your knowledge. It's a test of how well you work in team and your communication skills. Don't immediately assume the role of team leader because you think you know more - that is a one-way ticket to failing. Instead talk with your team until a solution presents itself. This is the bit which is hardest as everyone jumps at the team leader role because they think it will get them a place. Just whatever you do don't stay quiet. If you see someone else who is quiet, invite them in as a part of the team – not only will the interviewers like this, but it's the decent thing to do.

When the test comes to an end, the interviewers will ask you each to say a piece on the project. Don't try to take all the credit and don't be greedy with the spotlight. Try to compliment the team's ability.

After the interviewers have said you can go, make sure to congratulate your team as you walk out and to talk and keep talking with them as the day progresses. The assessors will be looking out for that.

Talking to Apprentices

It is common for there to be some people there who are in the second or third year of their apprenticeships. They are there to tell you "what it's really like" to be on the apprenticeship scheme.

Although they will not take part in any decision making processes, they will be asked for their opinions of the candidates. This means that their opinions may help to confirm the opinions of the interviewers in a borderline decision, but it is the interviewers who will make the real choices.

This means ask them questions. Things like, how much does accommodation cost? What are good areas to live? Is there a canteen, and if so, is it subsidised? How does it work with the study part of the apprenticeship? If you drive, then ask them about parking. They have knowledge, so access it.

Site Tour

If there is a site tour, then most likely it will be current apprentices that are taking you around. Ask relevant questions, but also allow others to ask questions. If you see someone struggling to get a question in because someone else is hogging the limelight, find a way of pushing them forward.

Time to state the obvious (again): Pay careful attention to any Health and Safety measures while on a site tour. Maybe it's a requirement for a hard hat, maybe it's a line you have to stand behind. Follow the rules.

Yes, I know that newspapers love to run headlines about "Health and Safety Gone Mad!!!"

I can tell you from what I have personally seen that safety rules are there to keep you safe. Ignoring safety rules gets you injured, possibly permanently. It may even get you dead.

Plus, if you're going to ignore Health and Safety, then you may as well go home, because there is no way you'll get the apprenticeship.

Lunch Break

At some point, there will be a break – maybe a coffee break, maybe for lunch, but there will be a break. Chat pleasantly, compliment other candidates.

And expect there to be a team sitting the other side of a partition listening to everything you do and say. Not every company does this, but a significant number do. So assume it is happening.

Self-criticism

This is not part of the face-to-face day, but it is something that you should always do afterwards. It is not about beating yourself up. It's about accepting that you're never going to be absolutely perfect, and that there's always room for improvement. If something went wrong, then work out how to fix it. If something went right, then work out why it was good, and apply it to the areas that were weaker.

It's like this: If you've got as far as a face-to-face interview, then you're good – very, very good. Even if you feel that it was a disaster, then the chances are that you're the only person who thinks that. You will still have put in a very creditable performance. The only people who don't put in a good performance are the ones who think that they can win the day through arrogance and attitude. For everyone else, you have to accept that you aren't going to get everything right, and look at how to do it better.

The most obvious reason for doing this (which hopefully you won't need) is in case you don't get the apprenticeship. In that case, facing up to what you didn't get right or could do better will help you with the next one.

There is a less obvious reason which will be covered in the next section.

Acceptance of an offer from an apprenticeship

Waiting for a call from the apprenticeship you are going for is the most stressful anxious feeling, but if you do get the apprenticeship, it's the best feeling in the world.

The Phone Call

First when you get the phone call answer the phone in a polite way, and do some basic pleasantries. When you are asked, "How do you think the interview went?" this is the make or break for getting the apprenticeship. It is not in the bag yet. You remember I said that you should always do self-criticism after a face-to-face (or any other interview for that matter)? Well, this is why.

You need to be able to say something along the lines of, "I think the interview went well, but there were things I could have done better, such as..."

For example, when I got my phone call the person on the phone said, "The interviewers were tough on the cohort this year and they thought some applicants did well and others not so much. How did you feel your personal interview and presentation went?"

I replied, "I think it went well and that the

presentation was good. I was able to get across what I wanted, but I could have done better on answering the questions."

The person responded by saying that the interviewers were very impressed by the presentation and thought I did well, but there aren't many places on the course. They then asked me how I thought the other applicants did and I gave them my opinion. This included a lot of good points but a few bad points. In this situation you have to make sure the good points outweigh the bad, otherwise it looks like you're throwing the other candidates under the bus. If you do that, then you won't get the apprenticeship.

After having said all that the chances that you got the apprenticeship are extremely high but continue to eat humble pie, as until you get the offer, then nothing's permanent. After having had a lot of talking hopefully they will then say something like, "We think you are a very good fit for the course and we would like to make you an offer."

When that happen, you can breathe a sigh of relief and celebrate. The people on the phones always like to hear the celebration because after a day of turning people down it makes them feel better.

On another apprenticeship offer that I received, the phone call was slightly different – as I have said before, every company does things differently. The person calling said, "Hello, I am calling to ask you how you thought your interview went and see what you thought about our interviewers."

This is tricky, partly because you can't say anything bad about them, but also because you have to make it believable. I said that they were very professional and knowledgeable and answered all the questions I had. I also said that they answered my questions about their projects when I showed an interest in them.

The person then moved on to the "How did the interview go?" question that I've already talked about.

There are other variations on this, and you may be asked questions on your knowledge of the organisation and what skills you hope to learn on the course. They may also ask what you will do to develop yourself after the interview. Don't make too many bad points about yourself but also don't set easy goals. You have to make it somewhere in the middle. After hearing you out, they might say what your good points were and even try to big you up and give you confidence. After all that, they will make an offer.

Say, "Yes."

What Do I Do With All the Notes I Made While Applying?

Keep them. All of them. Do not throw away anything to do with the apprenticeship you've just been offered.

Exam Results

It is quite possible that an offer will be dependent on getting certain exam results – for example, they might specify that you need to get at least 96 UCAS tariff points. Unlike universities, companies don't automatically get notified of your exam results, so you need to let them know. You will probably have to scan and e-mail them your results slip.

If your exam results turn out to be a disaster – talk to the company. They are likely to be a lot more reasonable than a university. Granted, at the end of the day, if you got Ungraded in every exam there's probably not a lot that can be done. On the other hand, if you're just a grade or two off – well, they've already put you through a selection process that's far tougher than the universities. At this stage, they have seen something in you that they want. They will also have invested a considerable chunk of money in you already during the selection process. Talk to them. See what they say.

Contracts

Sometime soon after you have accepted the offer, you will receive a written contract.

You might get some kid at school who thinks they're smart, telling you all about how if there's anything you don't like on there, then just cross it out, or that you can write your own terms on the contract, and things like that.

Ignore them. They're wrong.

The contract you're given is the only one you're going to get, and you have two choices: sign it or don't sign it. If you don't sign it, then you don't have an apprenticeship. Your choice.

My advice is to sign it.

Contracts do vary, but there's a few things that you can reasonably expect to see.

Start date and Job Title are two obvious ones, as is Salary. You will also expect to see where you will be based. This is important, because it's the area that you will have to look for accommodation (if it's too far away to live with parents).

The number of hours a week will also be included, although you should consider that a minimum rather than a maximum. You will end up working far more, especially when you add in the time for study and assignments. You will probably find a clause to the effect that, "Working patterns are subject to change at all times". People will try to be reasonable and considerate if you're asked to work anti-social hours, but all companies will expect a bit extra help if things go pear-shaped.

There will also be clauses relating to a probation period. This is common to all jobs, not just apprenticeships, so don't take it personally, or get paranoid. It amounts to everyone making sure that you're the right person for the job, and that you're happy with the job. During this period, reduced periods of notice will be in place.

There will be a lot of legalese, but the only other thing which will really make a difference to you is that it will tell you that your employment is for the duration of the apprenticeship (say, three or four years), and then if you successfully complete your training, they'll try and offer you a job. They won't give a definite guarantee of a job at the end of your apprenticeship, because no-one is able to see that far in the future. Still, it is pretty much a sure-fire thing – certainly as good a guarantee as anyone has, and a lot more certain than trying to find a job after following the standard university route.

Starting

Before Your Start Date

Before your start date, it is likely that you will get an invitation to a video conference with the rest of your cohort. This is a preview of what is going to happen. It gives you more of an idea of what to expect, and you may even get a timetable. You will also get introduced to the person who will be your main contact as an apprentice. They will have a title such as "Early Careers Development Officer", or "Apprentice Development Leader", or something like that. Make very sure that you get their e-mail address and phone number. They will be very important to you over the next few years.

Form Filling

Before your first day, you will fill in a lot of forms.

Remember when I said don't throw away any notes or information from the application process? Well, the chances are that you will need those notes now, and it will save you considerable effort if you've kept them.

It is legitimate for both the company you will be working for, and any education establishments they use to ask for a lot of personal information. I know that we have it drummed into us that you never give out personal information, but this is necessary.

Especially if you want to get paid.

In addition to signing a contract, the company will have some kind of "New Starters" form to fill in, which will include stuff like bank details and National Insurance number. It may also require the names of referees. It depends on what life experience you have before starting the apprenticeship who you use for a referee, but generally a teacher or college lecturer is fine.

You will also have to provide details such as next of kin.

If you are disabled, then you will have to fill in additional forms describing your disability, and any support needs that you might have.

With all these forms, just because you've told your employer something, that doesn't mean that the education provider (college or university) will have the information. Even if the company has told the education provider, do not expect that the information has got to the right person. I would be pleasantly surprised, if somewhat astounded if all the right people got the information they needed.

Never assume, "They already know that – I don't need to tell them again." Just fill the forms in. Again and again.

Your First Day

When you start your apprenticeship, you will probably have a team meeting with the rest of your cohort and the management team. This is a chance to get to know them before you start work.

When you attend this meeting always go in formal attire. If you overdress no problem and you know for next time. If you under dress then you look a bit out of place and give the impression that you couldn't be bothered.

When the meeting starts you will get an introduction and then you will have to introduce yourself. Keep it short and to the mark. For example, your name, what your hobbies are and where you are from. When the managers are talking pay close attention to all the information and take notes if you can. This meeting will probably be the first of many and this first one will affect you the most. It will probably include details of where you are studying and for how long the block release is, alongside your work, how will you get to your place of study, what will you be working on, your modules, your placements, your home base of operation, your mentors, where to find information and resources and where to look if you need help. Some of this information you will already have received, but up until this point, it will have been subject to change. Now it's what's going to be happening.

After the meeting take your notes and have a diary of what to do. This will really help you because there is a lot of information and a lot to take in. This will help keep you focused on doing one job at a time rather than try to do all of them at once and being overwhelmed. If you are struggling with the on boarding process, don't be afraid to ask your manager as they will help you out.

Valediction

I hope that this has given you useful information on how to go about getting an apprenticeship. It is not easy to get an apprenticeship. Once you have an apprenticeship, then there's a lot of hard work to complete it successfully.

Having said that, with the information in here you should be able to avoid some of the common pitfalls, and have a better idea of what you need to do.

As I have mentioned on many occasions, every company is different, and none are looking for quite the same thing. I covered all the standard tests, and told of some of the quirks that you might find. Still, there will be a company out there that will manage to come up with a completely different test, or do things in an odd order. They will have a good reason for doing things that way, so don't let it throw you. Expect that they will do something weird. Just take it in your stride and do the best you can.

I wish you well in your search for an apprenticeship.

About the Author

Joseph is a 20-year old apprentice. He wrote this book because when he was applying to become an apprentice, there was very little help around. Ultimately, he was offered four apprenticeships, three of which were from companies which are household names.

Away from his apprenticeship and writing, Joseph won an international art competition in 2008, and had his work displayed in the Mall Galleries, London. More recently, he was awarded the bronze medal for his category for Kata at the Jujitsu National Championships. He also spends his time playing guitar.

Printed in Great Britain
by Amazon

27202564R00046